MV√

PITTSBURGH
STEELERS

CREATIVE EDUCATION

JULIE NELSON

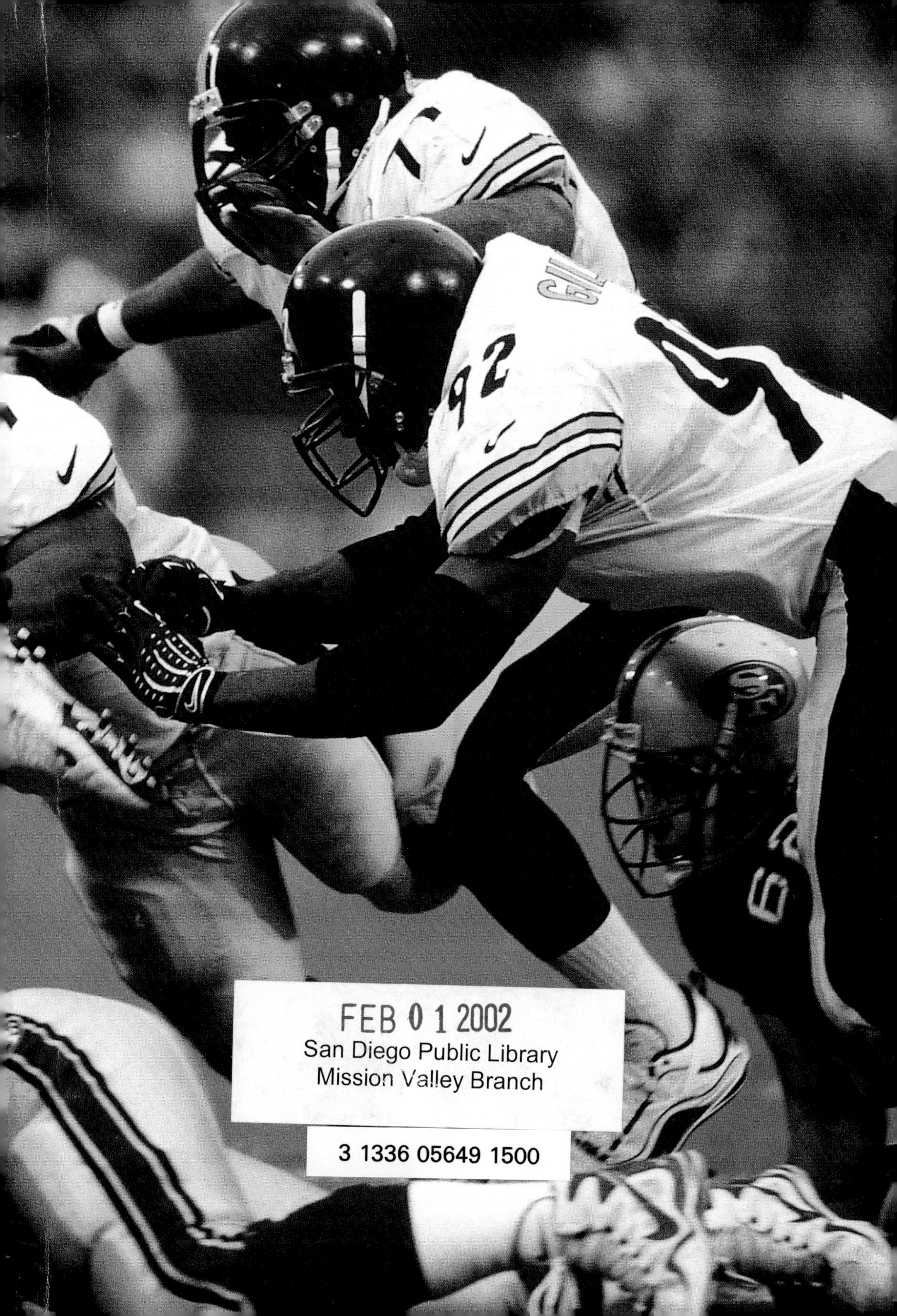
92

Published by Creative Education
123 South Broad Street, Mankato, Minnesota 56001
Creative Education is an imprint of The Creative Company

Designed by Rita Marshall

Photos by: Allsport USA, AP/Wide World Photos, Bettmann/CORBIS,
SportsChrome

Library of Congress Cataloging-in-Publication Data

Nelson, Julie.
Pittsburgh Steelers / by Julie Nelson.
p. cm. — (NFL today)
Summary: Traces the history of the team from its beginnings through 1999.
ISBN 1-58341-056-2

1. Pittsburgh Steelers (Football team)—History—Juvenile literature.
[1. Pittsburgh Steelers (Football team)—History. 2. Football—History.]
I. Title. II. Series: NFL today (Mankato, Minn.)

GV956.P57N45   2000
796.332'64'0974886—dc21   99-015754

First edition

9 8 7 6 5 4 3 2 1

In the early 1970s, Pittsburgh, Pennsylvania, went through a rebirth. Although work was slowing down at the local steel mills and unemployment was high, the people of Pittsburgh believed that there was more to their hometown than mills, buildings, and smoke. They knew that the city's most valuable resource was the community of people living there. So they began cleaning up their city and rebuilding it. Soon, Pittsburgh had been transformed into one of America's most livable communities.

During that same period, Pittsburgh's professional football team, the Steelers, was undergoing a rebirth of its own. For

An early star, rusher John Henry Johnson.

nearly 40 years, the Steelers had floundered near the bottom of the National Football League. Then, in the early 1970s, an innovative coach named Chuck Noll began rebuilding the Steelers' lineup around such future Hall-of-Famers as Terry Bradshaw, Franco Harris, Jack Lambert, and Joe Greene. Once Noll established a new winning attitude, the Steelers rose to the top of the league, capturing four Super Bowls in the years between 1975 and 1980.

1 9 3 3

Art Rooney established a pro football franchise in Pittsburgh, calling it the Pirates.

The newfound dominance of the Steelers was almost as remarkable as the turnaround of the city of Pittsburgh. It was fitting that the two success stories occurred together, since hard-working fans in the "Steel City" have always closely identified with their heroes in the black and gold uniforms.

ONE MAN'S DREAM

From the franchise's beginning in the 1930s, Pittsburgh football teams were noted for their hard-nosed effort but inability to win games. Only one man, Art Rooney, firmly believed that this could change.

Arthur Joseph Rooney was born in 1901, the eldest of nine children. As a young man, Rooney was a fine athlete and was signed to a baseball contract by the Boston Red Sox, but an arm injury ended his hopes of a playing career. Rooney was still determined to make sports his life, however, and he began exploring the idea of owning a team.

Two key events happened in 1933 that helped make Rooney's dream a reality. The first was the passage of a new Pennsylvania state law that permitted football games to be played on Sundays. The old law had kept Pittsburgh and

One of the NFL's most versatile athletes, Kordell Stewart.

Pittsburgh avoided going winless by beating Philadelphia in the final game of the season.

Philadelphia teams out of the NFL, which scheduled Sunday games. The second event involved a lucky bet that Rooney made at the Saratoga horse-racing track in New York. With his $2,500 in winnings, the young Irishman purchased an NFL franchise for Pittsburgh.

Rooney called his team the Pirates, after his favorite baseball team. He was certain that sports fans in Pittsburgh would support these football Pirates, too. After all, pro football had a long history in western Pennsylvania. Forty years before Rooney fielded his team, a former Yale star named Pudge Heffelfinger had been paid $500 to play for the Allegheny Athletic Association in the United States' first pro football game. In that game, Heffelfinger jarred the ball loose from an opponent, picked it up, and scored the winning touchdown.

Unfortunately, Rooney's team didn't have anyone with Heffelfinger's talent. His squad of young rookies and semipro veterans finished the 1933 season in last place in the NFL's Eastern Division with a 3–6–2 record. The team's play was embarrassing enough, but its uniforms were even worse. Rooney clad his players in striped jerseys that made them look like fugitives from a chain gang. Opposing players called them "jailbirds."

Rooney soon changed the uniforms, but he couldn't alter the team's fortunes. The Pirates didn't record a single winning season during the 1930s.

In 1941, Rooney brought in a new coach, Bert Bell, and changed the club's name to the "Steelers," in honor of the city's major industry. However, after watching a preseason workout, Rooney said, "Well, we've got a new team, a new coach, a new nickname, and new uniforms, but they look like the same old Pirates to me." Pittsburgh again finished in last place with a 1–9–1 record. Rooney dismissed Bell and brought back the team's former coach, Walt Kiesling.

Kiesling directed a remarkable turnaround in 1942, leading the club to its first winning record at 7–4. The Steelers' star that season was halfback Bill Dudley, who led the NFL in rushing. However, in 1943, Dudley and several other key players left Pittsburgh to serve in World War II, and the Steelers' record dipped below .500 again.

1 9 4 2

Rookie halfback Bill Dudley tore through defenses for a league-best 696 rushing yards.

A CHANGE OF LUCK

Walt Kiesling served three stints as coach in Pittsburgh, but few of those years were as successful as 1942. His last term was particularly disastrous for the Steelers' future. In 1955, Kiesling released a rookie quarterback named John Unitas during training camp. "Unitas can't remember the plays," Kiesling told Rooney. The Baltimore Colts, however, decided to give Unitas a chance. It turned out to be a good gamble, as he led the Colts to three NFL championships during a long Hall of Fame career.

After blowing their opportunity with Unitas, Pittsburgh's luck just had to change. In 1957, the club's fortunes did improve when Rooney picked Ray Parker as the Steelers' new coach. Parker, who had previously won three divisional titles with the Detroit Lions, concentrated on building an offense around quarterback Earl Morrall and receiver Jack Mc-Clairen. This talented combination led the Steelers to a 6–6 record in 1957. The next year, Parker made a trade to obtain Bobby Layne, who had quarterbacked Parker's best Lions

Two Steelers leaders of different eras, Terry Bradshaw . . .

. . . and cornerback Rod Woodson.

Tackle Gene "Big Daddy" Lipscomb played the final season of his Steelers career.

squads. Layne was a flamboyant star who played hard on Sunday afternoons and partied hard the rest of the week. He was also an outstanding competitor. "I never lost a game," he once told a reporter. "I just ran out of time."

Parker also made a key trade with the San Francisco 49ers, acquiring halfback John Henry Johnson to team with Layne in the Pittsburgh backfield. Johnson would go on to rush for more than 4,300 yards in six seasons in Pittsburgh to earn a place in the Hall of Fame. Parker's defense, meanwhile, was led by tackle Gene "Big Daddy" Lipscomb, a one-man wrecking crew.

With these stars leading the way, the Steelers posted five records of .500 or better in eight years. In Layne's last season with the team, 1962, Pittsburgh finished 9–5 and earned a postseason berth. The Steelers lasted only one round in the playoffs, however, falling 17–10 to the Detroit Lions.

In 1969, Rooney hired Baltimore assistant Chuck Noll as the club's 14th head coach. Noll had two things going for him: his football knowledge and his patience. He felt that the best way to build the Steelers would be slowly through the NFL draft. His first pick turned out to be one of the best in the club's history—a tall defensive tackle from North Texas State named Joe Greene. Greene's college teammates and opponents called him "Mean Joe," and his professional opponents soon learned why. "He didn't get that nickname because he liked to pick daisies," Redskins quarterback Joe Theismann once said. Noll also selected a second outstanding defensive lineman in the 1969 draft, L.C. Greenwood.

Noll's patience was tested that first season, as the Steelers won their opening game and then lost 13 straight. They did score one big victory after the season, however, winning the coin toss for the right to choose first in the 1970 NFL draft. With that pick, Noll selected quarterback Terry Bradshaw out of Louisiana Tech.

Like many Southern youngsters, Terry Bradshaw began playing football at an early age. As a child, he was small and skinny, and he had to constantly prove he was tough enough to play. In junior high, he was cut from the football team. But Bradshaw worked hard to improve his football skills and finally won the starting quarterback position on his high school team as a senior. He then proved he was ready to be a star by throwing for more than 1,400 yards and 21 touchdowns. Those statistics earned him a football scholarship to Louisiana Tech, a school 75 miles from his hometown of Shreveport.

1 9 6 9

L.C. Greenwood began a career that would end with a team-record 73.5 sacks.

Cornerback Mel Blount.

When Bradshaw graduated from college four years later, the once-skinny boy had become a 6-foot-3 and 215-pound man with a powerful arm. Every pro team wanted him, but Chuck Noll's Steelers got him.

1 9 7 0

John Fuqua led Pittsburgh's running attack with a club-record five yards per carry.

When Bradshaw reported to the Steelers' rookie camp, however, he felt as awkward as he had in junior high. He was lonely so far from home and trying too hard to do things right on the field. In his first professional game, Bradshaw misfired on nine straight passes and completed only four of 16 before Noll mercifully benched him. "The benching put a big lump in my throat," Bradshaw said. "I told myself, 'What now, big shot? Everybody was counting on you, and you blew it.'"

Bradshaw began to doubt himself during that tough first year. In desperation, he asked his college coach to send films from his college games. "I was trying to be Joe Namath or somebody, instead of being myself," he recalled. He decided then to concentrate on being Terry Bradshaw.

THE TEAM OF THE '70S

While Bradshaw was working through his problems, the Steelers' offensive line, anchored by center Ray Mansfield and tackle Jon Kolb, was beginning to jell. Noll knew that a solid line was vital to protect his young quarterback. But what the team really needed was a strong running game to balance Bradshaw's passing. Noll solved that problem by making Penn State fullback Franco Harris the Steelers' first-round draft choice in 1972.

"Franco was the key man on our ball club," teammate Joe Greene noted years later. "We were coming on every year in

Hall of Fame running back Franco Harris.

Legendary linebacker Jack Ham.

the 1970s, getting better and better. All we needed was the catalyst, and Franco was it."

After a slow start at the beginning of the 1972 season, Harris rushed for more than 100 yards in six straight games, tying what was then an NFL record. Led by Harris, the Steelers won nine of their last 10 games to capture the AFC Central Division title and earn their first playoff berth since 1962.

Harris saved his greatest play of the 1972 season for the end of Pittsburgh's playoff game against the Oakland Raiders. With only 22 seconds to go, Oakland was leading 7–6. Things looked pretty hopeless to Steelers fans, and Art Rooney left the owner's box at Three Rivers Stadium to go down and congratulate his players on their fine season.

Tackle Joe Greene led Pittsburgh's "Steel Curtain" defense with 11 quarterback sacks.

While he was in the elevator, Rooney could just make out the sound of the crowd roaring. He raced onto the sidelines, where he learned about Harris's miraculous play.

With the clock ticking down, Terry Bradshaw had rifled the ball toward halfback John "Frenchy" Fuqua, but Raiders defensive back Jack Tatum arrived at the same moment as the ball, crushing Fuqua with a ferocious hit. The ball bounced straight back toward Bradshaw like a rocket. Before it could hit the ground, however, Harris, who had been trailing the play, caught the ball near his shoe tops and outran Oakland defenders to the end zone for the winning touchdown. Harris's remarkable catch would go down in NFL history as "the Immaculate Reception."

Unfortunately, not even Franco Harris could stop the Miami Dolphins express the next week. The Dolphins edged the Steelers 21–17 in the AFC championship game on their way to an undefeated season and a Super Bowl win.

The Steelers are known for their bruising ground attacks (pages 18-19).

1 9 7 4

Intimidating line-backer Jack Lambert began his 11-year reign of terror in Pittsburgh.

Noll's draft-pick success reached its high point in 1974, when the Pittsburgh coach selected wide receivers Lynn Swann and John Stallworth, linebacker Jack Lambert, and center Mike Webster. Those players would eventually earn a combined 24 Pro-Bowl appearances and 16 Super Bowl rings.

Propelled by the success of the draft, Art Rooney's "Black-and-Gold" captured Super Bowl IX after the 1974 season. After 41 years, the Steelers had finally brought a championship to Pittsburgh. The big star of Pittsburgh's 16–6 win over the Minnesota Vikings was Franco Harris, who rushed for a record 158 yards, but the biggest winner was Art Rooney. "Today's win made all the other years worth it," said Rooney, his voice quivering with emotion. "I am happy for the coaches and players, but I'm especially happy for the Pittsburgh fans. They deserved this."

The Steelers didn't want to be known as one- or even two-year wonders, so they went out and captured three more Super Bowls during the next five years. They defeated the Dallas Cowboys 21–17 in Super Bowl X and 35–31 in Super Bowl XIII, then crushed the Los Angeles Rams 31–19 in Super Bowl XIV. Those victories earned the Steelers the title "the Team of the '70s."

Throughout the Steelers' championship years, the cast remained basically the same. Terry Bradshaw, Franco Harris, and Rocky Bleier starred in the backfield; wide receivers Lynn Swann and John Stallworth made countless acrobatic receptions; and linebackers Jack Lambert, Jack Ham, and Andy Russell, defensive backs Mel Blount and Donnie Shell, and linemen Joe Greene and L.C. Greenwood formed an impenetrable defense known as "the Steel Curtain."

As the Steelers entered the 1980s, the team's greats retired one by one. Coach Chuck Noll tried to rebuild by drafting young stars such as running backs Greg Hawthorne and Frank Pollard and quarterback Mark Malone on offense and linebackers Robin Cole, Mike Merriweather, and Dennis Winston on defense.

In 1983 and 1984, Pittsburgh captured AFC Central Division titles for the eighth and ninth times in 13 seasons. In the 1983 playoffs, they were trounced 38–10 by the Los Angeles Raiders. However, things looked brighter in 1984. The Steelers edged out Denver 24–17 to reach the AFC championship game against the Miami Dolphins. The new Steelers came up short in that contest, however, 45–28.

From there the Steelers' fortunes began to slide downward. The club failed to make the playoffs four straight years between 1985 and 1988. The two bright spots during those years were the play of Louis Lipps at wide receiver and Rod Woodson at cornerback. But the Steelers needed a quarterback.

To find their new field general, Rooney and Noll looked once again to Louisiana. Walter Andrew Brister III, known to friends as "Bubby," was a standout quarterback at Northeast Louisiana University. The Steelers made Brister their third pick in the 1986 NFL draft.

Brister made his first mark in the NFL during a game against Houston late in the 1988 season, tossing three touchdown passes to spearhead a 37–34 upset of the Oilers. From that performance, Brister's confidence began to grow. At the team's spring training camp in 1989, Bubby wrote the words

1 9 8 8

Frank Pollard rushed for a team-high 3,989 yards during the 1980s.

21

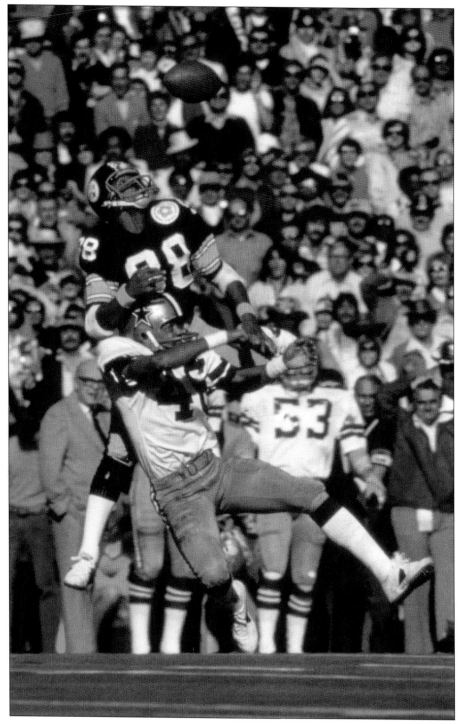

Graceful wide receiver Lynn Swann.

"PLAYOFFS 89" on a chalkboard. Then he went out to make his prediction come true. The Steelers won five of their final six games to return to the playoffs. Then, in a first-round game against Houston, Brister engineered another last-second drive to tie the contest and send it into overtime. A few minutes later, Gary Anderson's 50-yard field goal won the game for Pittsburgh, 26–23.

A narrow loss to Denver the following week ended Brister's storybook season, but Steelers fans were certain that better times were ahead in the 1990s. Unfortunately, Art Rooney would not be around to see them. The father of professional football in Pittsburgh for more than 55 years died just before the start of the 1989 season.

Bruising runner Barry Foster led the AFC with 1,690 rushing yards.

A RESURGENT DECADE

The new decade brought lots of changes for the Steelers, including several bright new stars. Before his retirement after the 1991 season, coach Chuck Noll drafted quarterback Neil O'Donnell, huge tight end Eric Green, and explosive halfback Barry Foster. Noll also left the defense in the able hands of such young stars as Rod Woodson, already considered one of the best defensive backs of all time, and ferocious linebacker Greg Lloyd.

Noll brought these players to Pittsburgh, but it was up to Pittsburgh native Bill Cowher, who took over the coaching reins in 1992, to mold them into a winning team. Cowher, a former NFL linebacker and defensive assistant coach, had grown up not far from Three Rivers Stadium. "I still remember registering him for Pop Warner football," said Cowher's

Rod Woodson was named the NFL Defensive Player of the Year.

father Laird. "Now that same boy is back home coaching the hometown team I've lived and died for my whole life. What a fairy tale." In his first year in Pittsburgh, Cowher was named NFL Coach of the Year after leading the Steelers to an 11–5 record and another Central Division title.

The Steelers made the playoffs again in 1993 and 1994 through brute force on both offense and defense, much like the legendary Pittsburgh teams of the 1970s. The club's fierce play prompted newspaper headlines such as "Back to the Future" and "Hard Hats Again."

The Steelers wanted another Super Bowl shot, and they came close in 1994. After rolling up an AFC-best 12–4 record and an NFL-best 55 sacks, the Steelers were confident they could drive all the way to Super Bowl XXIX in Miami.

Pittsburgh crushed Cleveland 29–9 in the first round of the playoffs and was a strong favorite against the San Diego Chargers in the AFC title game at home the following week. However, San Diego took a 17–13 lead with just over five minutes remaining. Chargers defenders then held off a desperate Pittsburgh comeback, breaking up a potential touchdown pass from O'Donnell to Barry Foster in the closing seconds to win the game and the conference title.

The following season, veteran receiver Yancey Thigpen emerged as a star, hauling in a club-record 85 catches. But the player who created the most excitement was rookie Kordell Stewart from Colorado. Stewart was drafted as a quarterback but excelled at other offensive positions as well. Coach Cowher gave him the nickname "Slash," because his position in the team program was listed as "quarterback/running back/wide receiver."

Cowher also designed new plays to make use of "Slash's" versatility. During one offensive series in a late-season game, Stewart, as quarterback, tossed a pair of passes to Thigpen and Mills. He then lined up at wide receiver, took a pitch from O'Donnell, and raced 22 yards for a touchdown.

These new offensive stars, plus the continued fine play of linebackers Greg Lloyd, Kevin Greene, and Levon Kirkland, helped the Steelers top Buffalo and Indianapolis in the playoffs to reach Super Bowl XXX. The hard-fought contest ended with the Dallas Cowboys on top, 27–17, but the game was really closer than the final score. Two misguided O'Donnell passes that wound up in the hands of Cowboys cornerback Larry Brown halted Steelers drives that could have won the game for Pittsburgh.

1 9 9 4

Coach Bill Cowher led the Steelers to a 12–4 record and the AFC Central championship.

RIDING "THE BUS" INTO THE FUTURE

After their Super Bowl loss, the Steelers regrouped for what would be a trying 1996 season. Defensive leader Greg Lloyd was injured in the season opener and lost for the season. Free agency also took a toll on the Steelers as Greene and O'Donnell moved on to other teams.

One new face in town was former St. Louis running back Jerome Bettis. At 5-foot-11 and 250 pounds, Bettis was a bruising runner known around the league as "the Bus." Although he had run for more than 1,000 yards in each of his first two years in St. Louis, he fell under criticism when his numbers dropped off in an injury-plagued 1995 season. The timing of his arrival in Pittsburgh was perfect for both parties. "I feel I have a lot to give to a team—positiveness,

Hard-hitting linebacker Levon Kirkland (pages 26-27).

Dominating center Dermontti Dawson was named to the Pro Bowl for the fifth straight year.

strength, and consistency on the field," Bettis explained. "That's the biggest thing. If you give me the football the same amount of times every game, I'll be consistent."

In his first season in Pittsburgh, Bettis delivered on that promise, carrying 320 times for 1,431 yards. Behind "the Bus," the Steelers captured their fourth AFC Central title in five seasons with a 10–6 record. They then headed into the playoffs with dreams of another Super Bowl. Unfortunately, after easily dispatching Indianapolis, Pittsburgh's hopes were dashed by a 28–3 loss to New England.

Pittsburgh continued to lose key defensive players in 1997, as Rod Woodson and Pro-Bowl linebacker Chad Brown departed as free agents. Offensively, Coach Cowher decided to make Stewart his full-time quarterback, and the

Powerful safety Carnell Lake.

move paid off. As Stewart threw for 3,020 yards and 11 touchdowns, Bettis tore through opposing defenses for 1,665 yards and seven touchdowns. Yancey Thigpen also continued to shine, piling up 1,398 receiving yards.

Boasting several of the AFC's top offensive weapons, Cowher's Steelers finished 11–5, earning yet another AFC Central Division title and the team's sixth playoff appearance in a row. In Pittsburgh's first playoff game, however, it was the defense that came up big, limiting the New England Patriots to just six points in a 7–6 Steelers win. A week later, Pittsburgh's season came to an end with a 24–21 loss to the Denver Broncos.

With a defense that had been continually stripped and overhauled over the previous three seasons, Cowher's Steelers were expected to rely heavily on their well-balanced offense in 1998. Unfortunately, Stewart suffered a second-year slump at the helm of the offense, and his confidence plummeted along with the Steelers' offensive output. "It's eating me up right now, to go through down times," the young quarterback said. "I'm trying to keep my composure, but this team is not used to losing."

By the end of the season, the Steelers were 7–9 and out of the playoff picture for the first time in Cowher's tenure. It also marked the first time Cowher's Steelers finished below the .500 mark.

Despite Stewart's problems in 1998, the Steelers remained confident that he was the player that would lead them back into the Super Bowl. Pittsburgh soon hired Kevin Gilbride as the team's new offensive coordinator in the hopes that he could better utilize Stewart's many skills. "If things break

1 9 9 9

Troy Edwards led all Pittsburgh receivers in catches (61) and receiving yards (714).

"The Bus," running back Jerome Bettis.

A defender in the "Steel Curtain" tradition, linebacker Earl Holmes.

Fans in the Steel City expected Jason Gildon to become a major run-stopping force.

down, you need to use your ability and make the play, and we didn't see enough of that last year from Kordell," explained director of football operations Tom Donahue. "If we don't take advantage of his unique skills, it is a big mistake on our part."

Unfortunately, Stewart continued to struggle in 1999 as he split time with Mike Tomczak at quarterback. With its passing attack sputtering, Pittsburgh lost seven of its last eight games to finish the year 6–10. Particularly frustrating for Pittsburgh fans was the team's home record. The Steelers, a team that had long prided itself on its home-field advantage, mustered only a 2–6 record in Three Rivers Stadium.

Although the Steelers have fallen in the standings in recent years, the Steel City has never been a town of quitters. Pittsburgh began rebuilding in the 2000 NFL draft by selecting huge receiver Plaxico Burress in the first round. With Burress and such stars as Jerome Bettis and linebacker Earl Holmes leading the way, Pittsburgh may soon regain its rightful place atop the AFC.